Reversible and Irreversible Changes: Yajoo and Majoo's Terrible, Magnificent Mess

Student ISBN 978-1-952346-45-3

By Harishankar Manikantan PhD, Jake Hunter, Beth Hunter, Aysha Imtiaz, Nicole Muir, and Grant Cowell.

Yajoo and Majoo's Terrible, Magnificent Mess written by Aysha Imtiaz and Jake Hunter Illustrated by Bella Hunter, Watercolors by Beth Hunter, India ink by Lilly Hunter

STEMTaught® **Grade 2**
Next Generation Science

2-PS1-4 Matter and Its Interactions: Construct an argument with evidence that some changes caused by heating or cooling can be reversed and some cannot.

Featured author:

Hi, my name is Hari. I grew up in India, where my favorite subjects in school were math and science. I use math to model and understand the complicated science of flowing liquids. Particularly, I like to study the physics of goopy fluids like shampoo, gel, mayonnaise, and paste. I am a researcher in Chemical Engineering at the University of California, Santa Barbara. I believe that even the simplest things around us can tell us a lot about how the complex world works — you just need to stay curious and ask the right questions.

Harishankar Manikantan

Postdoctoral Researcher, Chemical Engineering
University of California, Santa Barbara

Explore the Phenomenon!

Is the change reversible or not?

Ice cream isn't the only thing that can melt on a warm day. Many substances melt and freeze near room temperature. Observe coconut oil as it changes from a solid to a liquid and back again.

What you need:

- a bowl of ice water
- a bowl of warm water
- a resealable clear plastic bag
- a little coconut oil

Plastic bag

Ice

What you will do:

1. Put coconut oil in your bag and seal it.

2. Put your bag of coconut oil in ice water. Take the bag out frequently to feel and observe the coconut oil.

3. Put your bag in warm water. Touch and feel the bag to observe the changes that occur.

4. Put it back in the ice water and observe.

COOL

WARM

Color the bar on your thermometer to show the temperatures of your warm and cold water.

What is the temperature of your warm water?

| °F |
| °C |

100 —
90 —
80 —
70 —
60 —
50 —
40 —
30 —
20 —
10 —

What is the temperature of your cold water?

| °F |
| °C |

100 —
90 —
80 —
70 —
60 —
50 —
40 —
30 —
20 —
10 —

What happens when you put coconut oil in cold water?

_____

_____

_____

What happens when you put coconut oil in warm water?

_____

_____

_____

Can the changes to the coconut oil be reversed? Yes   No

Coconut oil comes from the coconut

Coconut oil is used for cooking and frying foods. You can use coconut oil to make French fries, to make popcorn and to fry shrimp. Heating or cooling coconut oil causes it to change form. When cool, coconut oil is a white solid. When warm, it becomes a runny liquid! The changes to the coconut oil are reversible because they can occur again if the temperature changes.

IT'S SONG TIME!

Get ready to sing and clap to a song about reversible changes! Sing these verses to the tune of **"I'm a Nut."**

Uncle's Coco Oil Song!

Put coco oil in the pot

Heat it up till it gets hot

It's liquid and it's very clear

You made a change, now give a cheer!

Heat it up (clap, clap)

Heat it up (clap, clap)

Heat it up (clap, clap)

Heat it up

Turn off the heat, now cool it down

It turns white, you start to frown

The change you made is now undone

Now, heat again, it's lots of fun!

Cool it down! (clap, clap)

Cool it down! (clap, clap)

Cool it down! (clap, clap)

Cool it down!

Sing and clap to my song!!!

Can the changes to the coconut oil be reversed? How do you know?

Think, Pair, Share!

Shave ice is delicious

Can you think of a better way to cool off than with a colorful, delicious shave ice? Shaved ice, or "shave ice" in Hawaii, is a little different from a snow cone. Instead of crushed ice, the ice is finely shaved using tools. The ice shavings are as delicate as a fresh blanket of snow.

Hawaiian shave ice is a yummy treat.

Think, Pair, Share!

A shave ice can melt. What other things can melt?

What do you call a warm shave ice?

Fruit punch!

How is a shave ice treat made?

It is fun to watch how shave ice is made. Let me show you how it is done!

Start with a block of solid ice! It is cold and hard. Can you find the ice block in the photo?

Put the solid ice block into the machine. When it spins, soft fluffy ice shavings come out the bottom. It looks like snow!

Next, a sweet syrup liquid is poured over the ice shavings.

Yum, yum!

What is a solid, a liquid and a gas?

A solid, a liquid and a gas are three states of matter. Many types of matter can become a solid, liquid or gas depending on the temperature.

A solid

You can hold a solid in your hand. A solid can be cut or broken. Ice is a solid.

Practice writing the word solid.

Solid

A liquid

A liquid can flow. It can slosh around. A liquid can take on any shape because it is so runny. Water is a liquid.

Practice writing the word liquid.

Liquid

A gas

A gas is very thin. Most often a gas is see through. Air is a gas

Practice writing the word gas.

Gas

Is it a solid, a liquid or a gas?

Place these cards when you identify solids, liquids and gases as you continue reading.

Solid	Liquid	Gas

Solid	Solid	Liquid	Gas

Solid	Solid	Liquid	Liquid

Solid	Solid	Liquid	Liquid

Solid	Liquid	Liquid	

What does a snowman eat for breakfast?

Frosted flakes!

9

Can you identify solids and liquids?

Which materials related to shave ice pictured here are solids, liquids, or gases?

The large ice block is frozen and hard.

The ice is ...

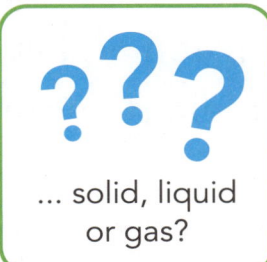

... solid, liquid or gas?

The tiny ice shavings are frozen and soft.

The ice shavings are ...

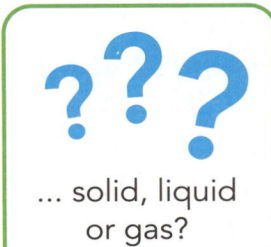

... solid, liquid or gas?

The sweet syrup pours out of a bottle.

The syrup is ...

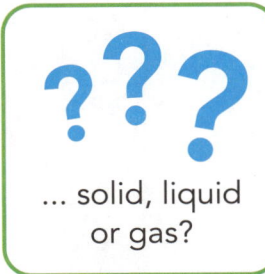

... solid, liquid or gas?

The shave ice melts in your mouth.

The melted treat in your mouth is ...

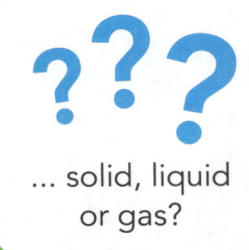

... solid, liquid or gas?

These melt if warm and freeze if cold

Ice cream begins as a creamy liquid. When the cream is frozen into a solid it becomes a delicious treat. Imagine a warm sunny day. As the ice cream warms up, it stops being frozen and firm. Now it flows and drips down the cone. It has melted back into a liquid again. This is a reversible change!

Warmer

Ice cream becomes melted when it warms up. Ice cream becomes frozen when it cools down.

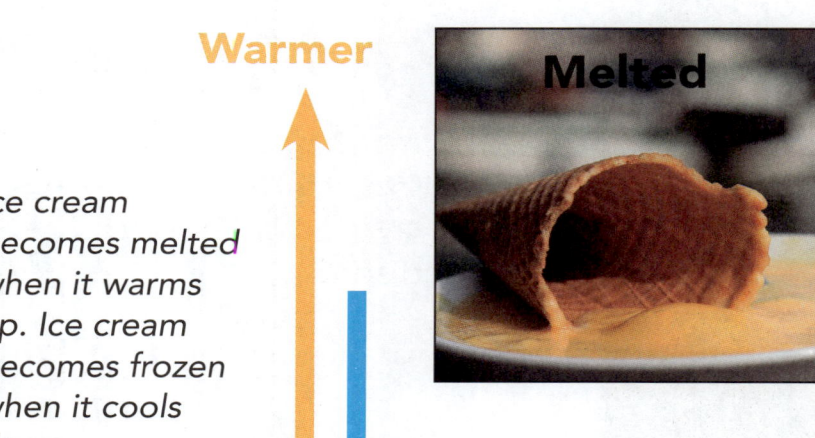

Melted

The melted ice cream is sticky and runny.

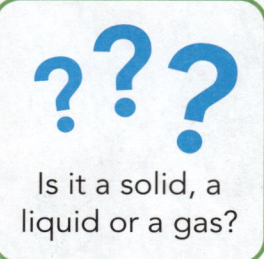

Is it a solid, a liquid or a gas?

Frozen

The frozen ice cream is firm and can be scooped.

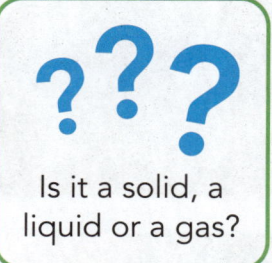

Is it a solid, a liquid or a gas?

Cooler

What can cause ice cream to melt? How could it become frozen again?

Think, Pair, Share!

Cut and fold to see what happens if you raise the temperature!

What happens when you warm butter?

What happens when you warm chocolate?

What happens when you warm coconut oil?

The cubes of butter are firm when cool.

The butter is a ...

??? Is it a solid, a liquid or a gas?

You can hold chocolate in your hand when it is cool.

The chocolate is a ...

??? Is it a solid, a liquid or a gas?

When coconut oil is cool, it freezes. You can scoop the hardened oil with a spoon.

The coconut oil is a ...

??? Is it a solid, a liquid or a gas?

When you heat the butter on the stove it melts.

The butter is now a ...

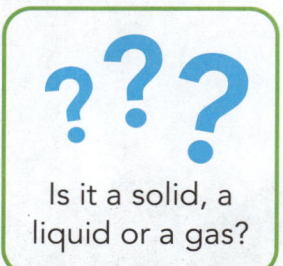

Is it a solid, a liquid or a gas?

When you heat chocolate on the stove it melts.

The chocolate is now a ...

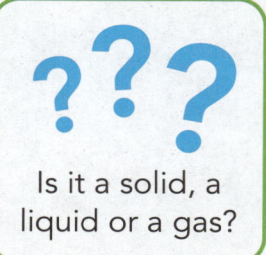

Is it a solid, a liquid or a gas?

When warmed, coconut oil melts and becomes clear and runny.

The coconut oil is now a ...

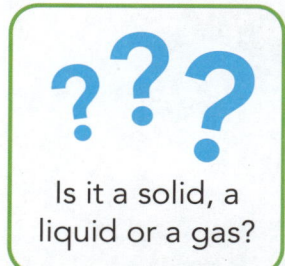

Is it a solid, a liquid or a gas?

Fold Line

14

Cut and fold to see what happens if you raise or lower the temperature!

What happens when you freeze water?

Ocean water is a good home for a swimming otter.

The water is a ...

Is it a solid, a liquid or a gas?

What happens when you hang the clothes in warm air?

When clothes are wet we hang them out to dry.

The water making the clothes wet is a ...

Is it a solid, a liquid or a gas?

What happens when you warm the ice?

When carbon dioxide gas freezes it becomes a hard white ice.

The carbon dioxide ice is a ...

Is it a solid, a liquid or a gas?

Ice in the frozen Arctic is a good home for a penguin.

The ice is a ...

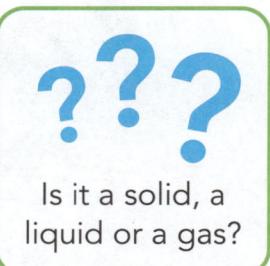

Is it a solid, a liquid or a gas?

When water evaporates it goes into the air.

The water vapor is a ...

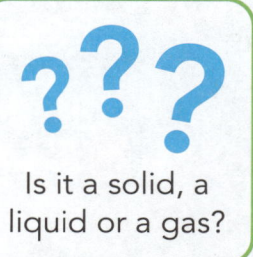

Is it a solid, a liquid or a gas?

When warmed, carbon dioxide ice becomes a cold white vapor.

Carbon dioxide vapor is a ...

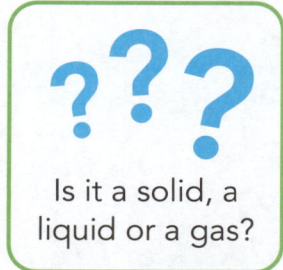

Is it a solid, a liquid or a gas?

When does coconut oil melt?

Different substances freeze, melt and boil at specific temperatures. Coconut oil becomes a solid at 78 °F (26°C) or lower. Above 78 degrees, it melts into a liquid.

Solid   Liquid

78°F

Cooler ←   → **Warmer**

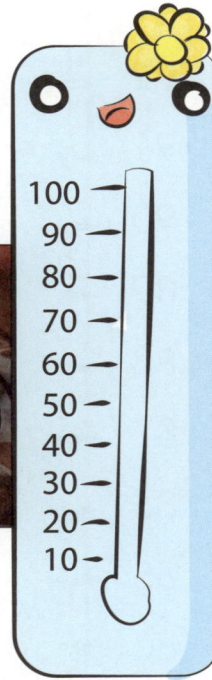

Color up to 78°F on your thermometer.

When does chocolate melt?

When liquid chocolate cools below 89°F (32°C) it becomes a solid. When chocolate is left out on a hot day above 89°F (32°C) it melts into a gooey liquid.

Solid   Liquid

89°F

Cooler ←   → **Warmer**

How does temperature affect coconut oil and chocolate? Are these changes reversible?

Think, Pair, Share!

Color up to 89°F on your thermometer.

Graph melting and freezing temperatures

These edible substances melt and freeze near room temperature. Graph their melting temperatures.

Substance	Melting/Freezing Temperature
Butter	93°F (34°C)
Chocolate	89°F (32°C)
Coconut oil	78°F (26°C)

Woof, woof!!!

When Butter, Coconut Oil and Chocolate Melt

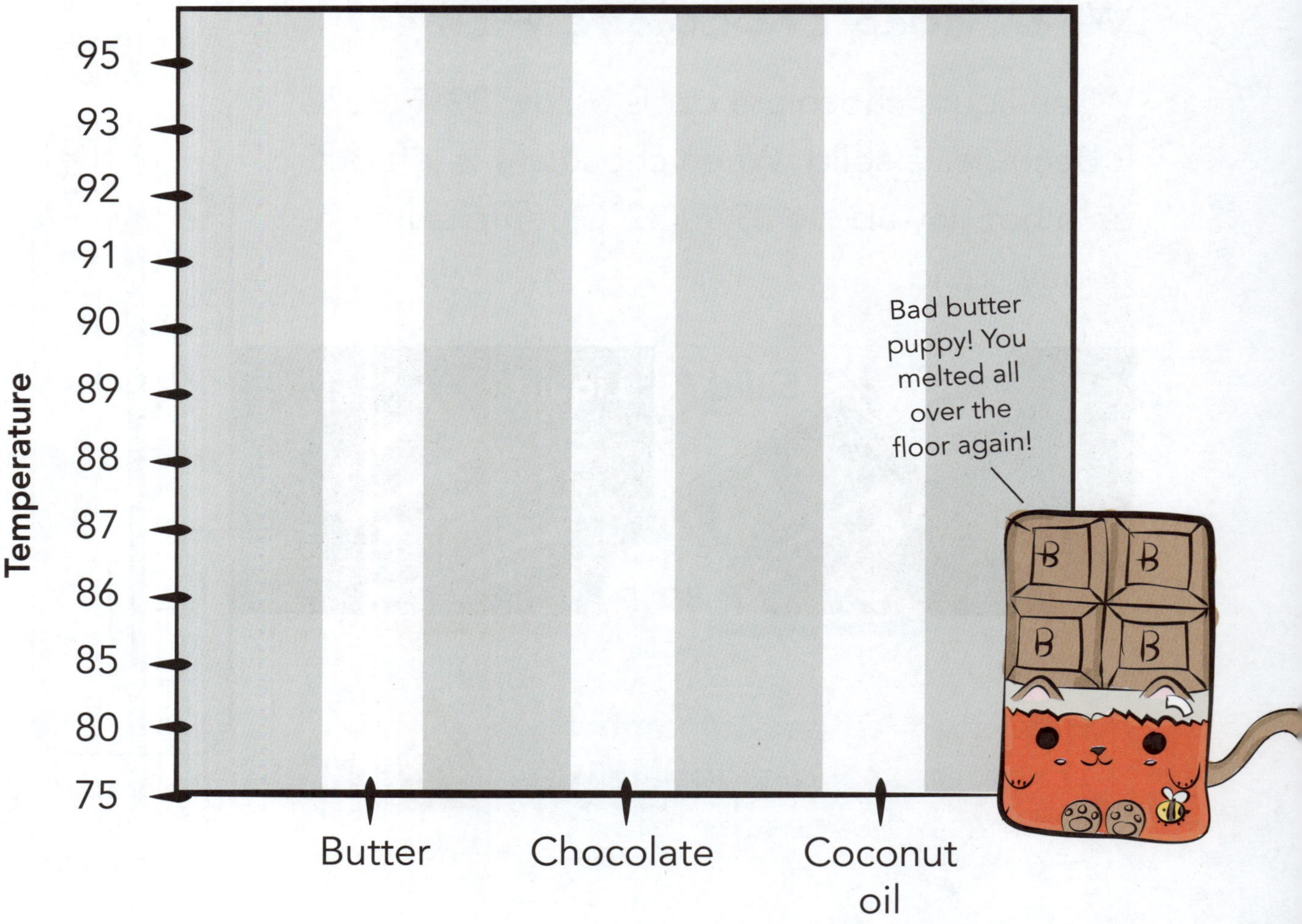

Temperature

95
93
92
91
90
89
88
87
86
85
80
75

Butter   Chocolate   Coconut oil

Bad butter puppy! You melted all over the floor again!

18

Use your graph to make a prediction

What is the temperature in the room you are in?

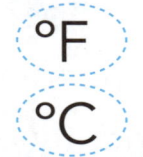 °F
°C

Color in your room's temperature on your thermometer.

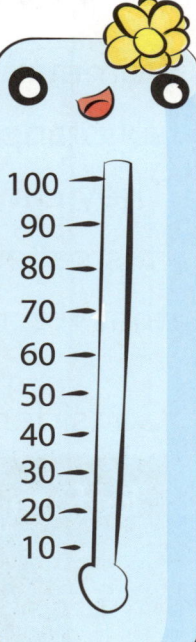

Which substances will be a solid and which should be liquid in your room right now?

_____

_____

_____

What is the temperature outside right now?

 °F
°C

Color in your room's temperature on your thermometer.

Which substances will be a solid and which should be liquid outside right now?

_____

_____

_____

Irreversible changes

Sometimes, when we heat or cool a substance, the changes are permanent! They can't be undone. When this happens it is called an <mark>irreversible change</mark>, meaning that the material has been permanently altered.

Consider a cooked egg ....

Before cooking (cold)

After cooking (hot)

What is an egg like before cooking?

_____

_____

_____

_____

What is an egg like after cooking?

_____

_____

_____

_____

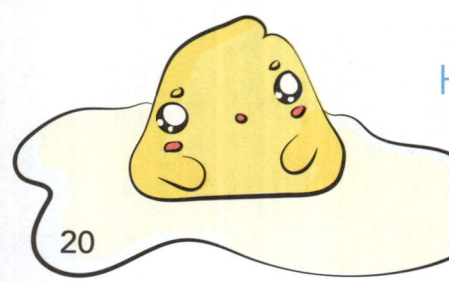

How does an egg change when it is cooked?

Think, Pair, Share!

A raw egg feels slimy and wet before it is cooked. It is a liquid. When heated on the stove, the egg becomes a solid. The egg does not become a liquid again when it cools. The change is irreversible!

Cut and fold the flaps to see more examples of irreversible changes.

No fair! Their change is permanent?

The raw meat is red and flexible.

What happens when you heat meat?

Fold Line

The marshmallows are white and soft.

What happens when you heat a marshmallow?

Fold Line

Irreversible changes

Some changes caused by heating or cooling can be reversed and some cannot. To know if a change is permanent, all you need to do is change the temperature and make observations. You can see if the material goes back to how it was or if the change is permanent.

When cooked over heat the meat turns brown.

Are the changes reversible or irreversible?  Think, Pair, Share!

How do you know?

Fold Line

When warmed over a fire the marshmallow turns brown and crispy.

Are the changes reversible or irreversible? Think, Pair, Share!

How do you know?

Fold Line

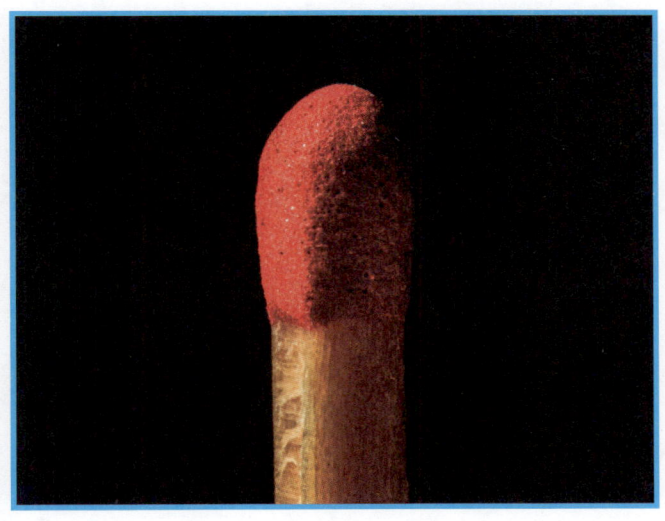

The match head is red and smooth.

What happens when a match is burned?

Fold Line

The pancake batter is a white runny liquid.

What happens when you heat pancake batter?

Fold Line

The spinach leaves are green and stiff.

What happens when you heat spinach?

Fold Line

23

When burned at a high heat, the match head becomes black and rough.

Are the changes reversible or irreversible?  Think, Pair, Share!

How do you know?

When heated on the stove, the pancake batter turns brown and becomes a solid.

Are the changes reversible or irreversible?  Think, Pair, Share!

How do you know?

When heated on the stove, the spinach becomes soft and limp.

Are the changes reversible or irreversible?  Think, Pair, Share!

How do you know?

Fold Line

IT'S SONG TIME!

Get ready to sing and clap to a song about an irreversible change! Sing these verses to the tune of **"I'm a Nut."**

Uncle's Fry the Egg Song!

Crack an egg into the pan

Cook it with a little Spam

The clear egg white runs all around

Don't cook too long or it turns brown!

Heat it up (clap, clap)

Heat it up (clap, clap)

Heat it up (clap, clap)

Heat it up

Turn off the heat, and cool it now

It tastes so good you eat it down

The change you made is here to stay

You like the egg when cooked this way!

Cool it down! (clap, clap)

Cool it down! (clap, clap)

Cool it down! (clap, clap)

Cool it down!

Sing and clap to our song!!!

YAJOO AND MAJOO'S
TERRIBLE, MAGNIFICENT MESS

By Aysha Imtiaz

Part 1

Yajoo and Majoo at your service

Yajoo and Majoo were the two cutest, but naughtiest, emus ever. If their father ever turned away, even for a split-second, they'd brew up all sorts of trouble. Yajoo and Majoo's mess making was relentless, and poor Father's house never looked the same from one day to the next.

Father was tired of their monkey business. He had gone out for a little stroll and returned to find ketchup splotches all over the walls! The ingredients in his kitchen were all mixed up. The twins had been making secret potions.

That night he had to scrub the floors and walls instead of reading stories to his baby emus. Father hoped this would teach them to never make a mess again.

The next morning, he left home to go help the neighbor. Yajoo and Majoo promised to be good.

Are ketchup splotches all over the wall a reversible or irreversible change?

Think, Pair, Share!

Then, Yajoo and Majoo had a great idea—a surprise for Father! Popcorn kernels were his favorite late night snack to munch on. He had a secret stash of popcorn kernels high up on the kitchen shelves.

Yajoo took his entire bottle of popcorn kernels and dumped it into a frying pan. Popping corn was flying everywhere! What little was left in the pan was blackened to a crisp. Thick smoke filled the room!

Majoo was busy using burnt kidney beans and rusty trinkets to make a "Bwoo-tee-ful" garland which he hung across the doorway as a decoration.

Is cooking popcorn on the stove a reversible or an irreversible change?

Think, Pair, Share!

Now it was time for the lava lamps! Yajoo had made these in school with Alka-seltzer, oil and water. Soon, dozens of colorful lava lamps gurgled and bubbled away. Sticky liquid dripped all over.

Next, he poured lemon juice and baking soda into his homemade volcano. The eruption frothed and fizzed and left a very sticky mess to clean up—but, Yajoo was just getting started! He had many more fun party activities planned!

Is reacting lemon juice with vinegar a reversible or an irreversible change?

Think, Pair, Share!

Meanwhile, Majoo was in the kitchen banging around and pecking at jar tops. He had accidentally tipped over the compost bin and tracked rotten fruit all over the floor.

He cracked eggs, measured and poured. He was making a special cake! He was so busy that he had left the milk out all morning and it was warm and going sour. He poured the milk into the batter, put in some birthday candles and loaded it into the oven.

After baking the cake, Majoo proudly opened up the oven door. Inside the oven was a smoky mess of burnt batter and melted wax.

What about the souring milk, rotten fruit and burnt cake? Are these reversible or irreversible changes?

Think, Pair, Share!

Then, the baby emus heard their father's footsteps coming up the walk. The twins quickly put mugs on top of their heads to use as party hats. They excitedly made identical squawking sounds when their father walked through the door.

When Father saw the mess, he gasped and stood there with his beak wide open. His adorable but naughty chicks just cocked their heads to the side and batted their long eyelashes like little angels. They seemed so proud of their mega-mess.

Why do you think Yajoo and Majoo were proud of their big mess? Have you ever made a big mess before?

Think, Pair, Share!

Father began scolding the twins as he looked around at all the damage. Yajoo had rearranged all the furniture in the room. He had stacked all the kitchen chairs into a pyramid. He had scribbled pictures of his favorite cousins, aunts and uncles on the wall as a party guest list.

Father started to put the furniture back into its place and then he looked down. His perfectly clean carpet was a sopping wet mess. Yajoo just smiled. He had hoped father would like it.

What about the wet carpet? Is this a reversible or an irreversible change?

Think, Pair, Share!